I0408971

CONTENT MARKETING SECRETS

Unlock the Power of Storytelling

Ray Goodwin

Copyright © 2023 Ray Goodwin

All rights reserved

The information contained in this book is intended for educational and informational purposes only. The author and publisher do not accept any liability for actions arising from the content of this book or for any errors or omissions. Readers are encouraged to seek professional advice before engaging in any activities or making any decisions based on the information contained in this book.

The views expressed in this book are those of the author and do not necessarily reflect the views of the publisher. The author and publisher make no representation or warranties of any kind with regard to the accuracy, completeness, or suitability of the information contained in this book for any purpose.

No part of this book may be reproduced, or stored in a retrieval system, or transmitted in any form or by any means, electronic, mechanical, photocopying, recording, or otherwise, without express written permission of the publisher.

ISBN-13: 9798852498212

Cover design & images by: Ray Goodwin

CONTENTS

LIABILITY DISCLAIMER

The information contained within this book is intended for informational purposes only and should not be construed as legal or professional advice. The authors and publishers of this book are not responsible for any losses or damages that may arise from the use of the information contained within.

The reader assumes full responsibility for any decisions made based on the information in this book. The authors and publishers do not endorse any particular method, service or product mentioned in this book and are not responsible for any consequences resulting from their use.

The reader should exercise caution and discretion when making life changing decisions, and should be aware of the risks and potential consequences of their actions. This book is not a substitute for professional or legal advice and should not be relied upon as such.

By reading and using the information in this book, the reader acknowledges and agrees to hold harmless the authors, publishers, and any other parties involved in the creation or distribution of this book from any and all liability, claims, damages, or losses that may arise from their use of the information contained herein.

CHAPTER 1: INTRODUCTION TO CONTENT MARKETING

In today's digital world, businesses are presented with endless opportunities to connect with their target audience. However, this level of connectivity has given rise to a new challenge – standing out from the competition. That's where content marketing comes in. By providing valuable, relevant, and consistent content, businesses can attract and retain a clearly defined audience and create a profitable customer base.

This book is jam-packed with practical advice, strategies, and insights based on my own experiences as well as those of other successful marketers who have cracked the code when it comes to content marketing. It doesn't matter if you are starting from scratch or looking for ways to improve your current content marketing efforts, this book will help you navigate the ever-changing landscape of online marketing.

Throughout this book, I will take you step-by-step through the process of creating compelling content that engages your audience and drives results. From understanding your target audience to crafting killer headlines that grab attention, you'll learn everything you need to know about creating high-quality content that resonates with your readers.

So what are you waiting for? Let's dive into the world of content marketing together and unlock the secrets of success!

What is Content Marketing?

Content marketing is a strategic marketing approach focused on creating and distributing valuable, relevant, and consistent content. Unlike traditional marketing tactics, such as print ads and commercials, content marketing aims to educate, entertain, or inspire the audience rather than aggressively promoting a product or service.

Content marketing is not a one-time campaign; it's more of a long-term approach to building a relationship with customers by providing helpful and informative content. Content marketing may include blog posts, infographics, podcasts, videos, e-books, webinars, social media updates, and more. The goal is to provide high-quality content that resonates with the needs and interests of the target audience.

Importance of Content Marketing in Digital Marketing

With the proliferation of social media and mobile devices, content marketing has become critical for businesses to succeed in the digital era. According to the Content Marketing Institute, 91% of B2B marketers use content marketing to reach customers. Meanwhile, 86% of B2C marketers consider content marketing an essential strategy.

The reason for this widespread adoption is that content marketing helps businesses to:

❖ Build a loyal customer base: By providing valuable content, businesses can establish themselves as a thought leader in their industry. This, in turn, helps build credibility and trust with the audience, making them more likely to choose the business over competitors.

❖   Improve brand awareness: Content marketing is an excellent way to showcase a brand's values, products, and services. By distributing content across different channels, businesses can increase brand awareness and encourage potential customers to consider them.

❖   Boost SEO: Creating high-quality content that is optimized for search engines can improve a brand's search engine rankings. This can give them better visibility in search results, increasing the chances of being discovered by potential customers.

Overview of the Different Types of Content Marketing

There are many types of content marketing, each with its unique set of benefits. Some of the most popular forms of content marketing include:

➤   Blogging: Blogging is a tried-and-true content marketing strategy that helps businesses build credibility, engage with their audience, and drive traffic to their website.

➤   Video Marketing: Video marketing is becoming increasingly popular, with businesses creating short videos to educate, entertain, or inform their audience.

➤   Infographics: Infographics present complex information in a visually appealing way, making them easy to understand and share.

➤   E-books: E-books are longer-form content that provides a more in-depth understanding of a particular topic. They are often used as a lead magnet, providing value in exchange for a potential customer's contact information.

➤   Podcasts: Podcasts are audio content that businesses use to build relationships with their audience and establish themselves as thought leaders.

Examples of Successful Content Marketing Campaigns

The most successful content marketing campaigns get people talking and sharing the content. Here are a few examples of businesses that have nailed their content marketing efforts:

❖   Red Bull: Red Bull's "Stratos" campaign was one of the most talked-about content marketing campaigns of all time. The energy drink brand sponsored Felix Baumgartner's record-breaking freefall from the edge of space. The event generated massive media coverage and social media buzz, making it one of the most successful content marketing campaigns in history.

❖   Dove: Dove's "Real Beauty" campaign aimed to empower women by challenging stereotypes and unrealistic media ideals of beauty. The campaign spanned across different channels, including social media, video, and print ads.

❖   HubSpot: HubSpot's content marketing efforts are world-renowned, with the company creating guides, blog posts, and webinars that help businesses improve their digital marketing efforts.

The Benefits of Content Marketing for a Business

Content marketing offers numerous benefits for businesses, including:

➢   Increased traffic: High-quality content can help increase website traffic, leading to more leads and customers.

➢   Improved SEO: Content marketing can help businesses rank higher on search engine results pages by providing valuable content that matches user intent.

➢   Cost-effective: Compared to other marketing strategies, content marketing is relatively inexpensive and can produce long-term results.

➤ Improved engagement: By providing valuable content, businesses can engage with their audience, improving brand trust and loyalty.

The Challenges of Content Marketing

However, content marketing is not without its challenges. Some of the major barriers businesses face when it comes to content marketing include:

❖ Limited resources: Creating high-quality content can be time-consuming and require significant resources.

❖ Measuring effectiveness: It can be challenging to measure how effectively a content marketing campaign is performing.

❖ Short attention spans: With so many options for content consumption, businesses must create content that grabs attention and provides value.

❖ Limited distribution: Even the most compelling content won't be successful if it doesn't reach the right audience.

The Objective of This Book

This book aims to guide businesses through the process of creating a successful content marketing strategy. From understanding the audience to measuring performance, each chapter of this book will provide actionable insights and strategies that businesses can use to elevate their content marketing efforts.

Summary

Content marketing is an incredibly effective way for businesses to connect with their audience and build a loyal customer base. By providing high-quality content tailored to the needs and interests of the audience, businesses can establish themselves as industry leaders, improve brand awareness, and boost SEO. While content marketing does come with its challenges, businesses that understand how to create and distribute valuable content will reap the rewards of increased traffic, engagement, and customer loyalty.

CHAPTER 2: UNDERSTANDING YOUR AUDIENCE

As the saying goes, "Know your audience." This is especially true in content marketing, where creating content that resonates with your target audience is crucial. In this chapter, we will discuss the importance of audience research, how to conduct it, and how to use the data to create audience personas and tailor your content to your audience.

Importance of Audience Research in Content Marketing

Audience research is a critical first step in any successful content marketing strategy. It helps you understand your target audience's needs, preferences, pain points, and motivations. This valuable insight helps ensure that the content you create is relevant, valuable, and engaging to your audience.

Without audience research, you risk producing content that misses the mark, wasting both time and resources, and damaging your brand's reputation. You may also fail to connect with potential customers, resulting in poor lead generation, conversion rates, and revenue.

Different Ways to Conduct Audience Research

There are several ways to conduct audience research, and the method you choose will depend on your budget, resources, and objectives. Here are some of the most common methods:

- ❖ Online Surveys - Online surveys are a popular method for gathering data about your audience's demographics, motivations, preferences, and behaviours. You can conduct surveys using online tools such as SurveyMonkey, Google Forms, or Typeform. Make sure your questions are clear, concise, and relevant, and offer an incentive, such as a discount or a chance to win a prize, to encourage participation.

- ❖ Social Media Listening - Social media platforms provide a wealth of data about your audience's interests, conversations, and preferences. You can use tools like Hootsuite, Sprout Social, or Brandwatch to monitor mentions of your brand or industry keywords, identify trends, and gain insights into your audience's needs and concerns.

- ❖ Focus Groups - Focus groups are an in-person or online gathering of a small group of individuals who represent your target audience. You can ask them questions, gauge their reactions to your content, and get feedback on your messaging. Focus groups can be costly, but they provide valuable qualitative data that can help you refine your content.

- ❖ Website Analytics - Your website analytics can provide key insights into your audience's behaviour and preferences. You can use tools like Google Analytics to track metrics such as page views, bounce rates, time on site, and conversion rates. This data can help you understand which content resonates with your audience and adjust your strategy accordingly.

How to Analyse Your Audience Data

Once you have gathered your audience data, the next step is to analyse it to extract insights and develop audience personas. Here are some tips on how to do it:

❖ Look for Patterns and Trends - Identify patterns and trends in your data. For example, do you see common demographic traits or interests among your audience? What are the most popular topics or formats for your content? These patterns and trends will help you develop a better understanding of your audience's needs and preferences.

❖ Develop Audience Personas - Use your data to create audience personas, which are fictional representations of your ideal customers. Audience personas include demographic information, pain points, motivations, interests, and communication preferences. Developing audience personas will help you create content that resonates with your target audience and guide your content strategy.

❖ Identify Content Gaps - Review your content to identify gaps in your audience's needs and preferences. Are there topics or formats that you're not covering? Are there pain points that you're not addressing? Use this insight to develop content that fills these gaps and better serves your audience.

How to Create Audience Personas and Use Them in Content Creation

Once you have developed your audience personas, you can use them to create content that speaks directly to your ideal customers. Here are some tips on how to do it:

❖ Tailor Content to Your Audience's Needs - Create content that addresses your audience's pain points, answers their questions, and provides value. Use the language and tone that resonates with your audience and highlights how your products or services can help them.

❖ Consider Your Audience's Communication Preferences - Different audiences prefer different communication channels and formats. For example, younger audiences may prefer video content, while older audiences may prefer email newsletters or blog posts. Use your audience personas to determine which channels and formats are most effective for reaching and engaging with your target audience.

❖ Use Personalization - Tailor your content to your audience's specific needs and preferences. Use their names, reference their previous interactions with your brand, and suggest content or products that align with their interests. Personalization can improve engagement and build a stronger connection with your audience.

Tips for Tailoring Content to Your Audience

Here are some tips to help you tailor your content to your audience:

➢ Use Language and Tone that Resonates - Use language and tone that speaks directly to your audience and aligns with their preferences. For example, if your audience is young and informal, use a conversational tone and avoid jargon or technical terms that may be difficult to understand.

➢ Address Pain Points and Needs - Create content that addresses your audience's pain points and needs. Identify their challenges and offer solutions that highlight the benefits of your products or services.

➢ Use Different Formats and Channels - Use different content formats and channels to appeal to your audience's preferences. For example, you can use video, podcasts, infographics, blog posts, email newsletters, or social media posts to reach your target audience.

Strategies for Engaging and Building Trust with Your Audience

Here are some strategies to help you engage and build trust with your audience:

- ❖ Provide Value - Create content that provides value to your audience. Offer tips, insights, or solutions to their problems. This will help build a positive association with your brand and demonstrate your expertise in your field.

- ❖ Respond to Feedback - Respond to feedback from your audience and address any concerns or questions they may have. This will show that you value their opinion and are committed to improving their experience with your brand.

- ❖ Share User-Generated Content - Share user-generated content on your social media platforms or website. This will show that you value your audience's contributions and help build a sense of community around your brand.

Summary

In this chapter, we discussed the importance of audience research in content marketing and how to conduct it. We covered the different ways to gather audience data, how to analyse it, and how to use it to create audience personas and tailor your content to your audience's needs and preferences. We also gave tips for engaging and building trust with your audience through content marketing. In the next chapter, we will discuss the importance of developing a content strategy and how to create one that aligns with your business goals and audience needs.

CHAPTER 3: DEVELOPING A CONTENT STRATEGY

In today's fast-paced digital world, having a content strategy is essential for any business seeking to improve its online presence and engage with its audience. A content strategy is a roadmap that outlines the types of content you will produce, the channels you will use to distribute them, and how you will measure and track your content's performance. A well-defined and executed content strategy can help you establish authority in your industry, build trust with your audience, and increase your website's traffic and conversions.

Importance of Having a Content Strategy

Having a content strategy is essential because it enables you to align your content with your business goals. A comprehensive content strategy will also help you anticipate your audience's needs and preferences, enabling you to create content that resonates with them.

Creating a content strategy also ensures that your efforts are consistent and cohesive. When you have a plan in place, you can avoid creating content that's not aligned with your brand's voice or tone. This consistency in your content will help your audience recognize you and establish familiarity with your brand.

Tips for Developing a Content Strategy

❖ Define Your Goals: Determine what you want to achieve with your content marketing efforts, whether it is to drive traffic to your website, generate leads, build brand awareness, or establish yourself as a thought leader in your industry.

❖ Define Your Brand Voice and Tone: Establish your brand's personality and how you will communicate with your audience through your content. Will your brand voice be playful or formal? Will it be informative or entertaining?

❖ Create a Content Calendar: A content calendar helps you plan and organize content creation, ensuring that you're consistently producing content. Choose a time frame such as weekly or monthly and create deadlines for each piece of content.

❖ Determine the Best Channels for Your Content: Assess the channels that your audience uses most frequently and focus on creating content that's tailored to that channel. For instance, if your audience is most active on Instagram, create visual content that will capture their attention.

❖ Measure and Track Your Content Performance: Use analytics tools to measure the success of your content strategy, such as the number of views, shares, and engagement rates. Use the data insights gained to continually optimize your content strategy.

How to Set Content Marketing Goals

When setting content marketing goals, it's essential to keep them SMART: Specific, Measurable, Attainable, Relevant, and Time-Bound. Have a specific and measurable goal that aligns with your business objectives. Ensure your goal is attainable, depending on your resources and budget. Ensure your goal is relevant to your audience's needs and is time-bound, giving a deadline for when you expect to achieve it.

How to Define Your Brand Voice and Tone

Your brand voice and tone will form the foundation of your content strategy. The voice is the overall personality of your brand while the tone is the emotional inflection of your copy. The first step in defining your brand voice is developing your brand's personality. Make it as detailed as possible to ensure clarity and consistency in your voice. Define three to five adjectives that describe your brand. For example, your brand personality might be friendly, sophisticated, and informative.

Once you have established your brand personality, define your tone of voice. Your tone should reflect how you want your audience to feel when they engage with your content. Ask yourself, what emotion do you want your audience to feel? Your tone should align with your brand personality and be consistent across all your content.

How to Create a Content Calendar

A content calendar will help you plan and organize your content better. Start by determining the frequency of your content publication and creating a schedule around it. Your schedule should include key events, holidays, and seasonally relevant content. Ensure you add deadlines to your content creation process, and assign tasks to team members when necessary.

When creating your content calendar, consider the type of content you want to produce. For instance, blog posts, social media posts, infographics, or videos, among others. Also, consider the channels you want to use to distribute your content. Establish a mix of channels that your audience uses most frequently.

How to Determine the Best Channels for Your Content

The type of content you produce will determine the best channels to use for distribution. For example, if you produce visuals like infographics, you might want to consider Pinterest, Instagram, and Facebook. In contrast, if you produce long-form blog posts, Twitter might not be the best platform to host it.

Consider the channels where your audience spends most of their time and how they prefer to consume content. Always aim to create content that can be utilized on various channels and make it engaging and shareable.

How to Measure and Track Your Content Performance

There are many analytics tools available to track and measure your content's performance. Google Analytics is free, easy to use, and provides in-depth analytics on your website, enabling you to track how visitors engage with your content. You can use Google Analytics to track website traffic, bounce rate, average time on page, and conversions.

Social media analytics can provide insights into how your content performs on different channels. The analytics will provide information such as engagement rates, audience demographics, and the best time to post. Leverage the insights gathered from analytics to make data-driven decisions to improve your content strategy.

Summary

Creating a content strategy is an essential step in content marketing. A comprehensive content strategy takes into account your business objectives, brand voice, target audience, and content channels. The strategy should align with all other marketing efforts and regularly monitored and optimized. When you have a well-developed content strategy in place, it becomes easier to create relevant and engaging content that will connect with your audience.

CHAPTER 4: CREATING COMPELLING CONTENT

Creating compelling content is essential for any content marketing strategy, as it is what drives engagement and conversions. In this chapter, we will explore the characteristics of compelling content, how to brainstorm content ideas, types of content that resonate with audiences, how to create a consistent and cohesive brand story, how to write effective headlines and titles, the importance of visuals in content marketing, and how to optimize your content for search engines.

Characteristics of Compelling Content

Compelling content is content that resonates with your audience, captures their attention, and motivates them to take action. It needs to be informative, educational, entertaining, or inspirational - depending on the type of content and its objective. Here are some characteristics of compelling content:

❖ Relevant: It needs to be relevant to your audience's interests, needs, and challenges.

❖ Engaging: It needs to be interesting, entertaining, or emotional enough to capture your audience's attention and keep them engaged.

❖ Useful: It needs to provide value and solutions for your

audience's problems or questions.

❖ Authentic: It needs to be authentic and genuine, reflecting your brand personality and values.

❖ Credible: It needs to be credible and trustworthy, backed up by research, data, or authoritative sources.

❖ Unique: It needs to stand out from the other content out there, providing a unique perspective or angle.

❖ Actionable: It needs to motivate your audience to take action, whether it's to learn more, share it, comment, or purchase your product or service.

How to Brainstorm Content Ideas

Brainstorming ideas for content can be challenging, especially if you're not sure where to start or what your audience wants to see. Here are some tips for brainstorming content ideas:

❖ Research your audience's interests and challenges: look at what topics they're discussing on social media, forums, and comment sections. Use tools like Google Trends, Buzzsumo, or Quora to find trending topics and questions related to your industry.

❖ Analyse your competitors' content: What topics or formats are they covering? What are their most popular content pieces? Use this information to create your unique angle or to cover the topics they're missing.

❖ Use internal resources: Are there any internal experts or departments that can provide valuable insights and knowledge that you can translate into content? Interview them or use their data to create informative content.

❖ Follow current events and trends: Stay up-to-date on current events, holidays, or trends that are relevant to your industry. Use these as inspiration for content ideas.

❖ Use content tools: Tools like Hubspot's Blog Idea Generator, Answer the Public, or Google's Autofill can help you generate relevant and unique content ideas.

Types of Content That Resonate with Audiences

There are numerous types of content that you can create to fulfil different objectives and appeal to different audience preferences. Here are some types of content that are proven to resonate with audiences:

❖ Blog posts: informative, educational, and shareable blog articles that cover a wide range of topics.

❖ Infographics: visually appealing images that present complex data or information in an easy-to-understand format.

❖ Videos: engaging and emotional videos that tell your brand story, demonstrate your product or service, or provide educational value to your audience.

❖ Webinars: online presentations or workshops that provide educational content to your audience and can generate leads or sales.

❖ Ebooks: comprehensive guides or resources that dive deep into topics related to your industry or product niche.

❖ Case studies: in-depth analyses of your customers' success stories, showcasing how your product or service helped them achieve their goals.

❖ Social media posts: visually appealing, shareable posts that promote your brand personality, facilitate engagement, or provide informational or entertaining content.

❖ Podcasts: audio recordings of interviews, discussions, or

educational content related to your industry or niche.

How to Create a Consistent and Cohesive Brand Story

Crafting a consistent and cohesive brand story is crucial for building trust and loyalty with your audience. Your brand story should encompass your brand values, personality, mission, and unique selling proposition. Here's how to create a consistent and cohesive brand story:

- ❖ Define your brand values: What are the core values that drive your brand's decisions and messaging? Make sure they align with your audience's values and resonate with them.

- ❖ Develop your brand personality: What is the tone, style, and voice of your brand? Is it informal, humorous, serious, authoritative, or other? Make sure it reflects your target audience's preferences and expectations.

- ❖ Craft your brand messaging: What is your brand's mission statement? What is the unique selling proposition that sets you apart from your competitors?

- ❖ Develop your brand visual identity: What are the colours, logos, fonts, and design elements that represent your brand? Make sure they're consistent across all your content and channels.

- ❖ Create a story arc: Based on your brand messaging and values, create a story arc that spans across your content and connects with your audience on an emotional level. Make sure it's consistent and coherent, telling a story that resonates with your audience and motivates them to engage with your brand.

How to Write Effective Headlines and Titles

Writing effective headlines and titles is an essential skill for creating engaging and shareable content. Your headline or title is the first thing your audience will see, and it needs to capture their attention, arouse their curiosity, and motivate them to read or watch your content. Here are some tips for writing effective headlines and titles:

❖ Be concise: Keep your headline under 70 characters to ensure it's fully displayed on search engines and social media.

❖ Use strong verbs: Start your headline with an action verb that conveys the benefit or solution your content provides.

❖ Use numbers or digits: Numbers and digits can make your headline stand out and offer your audience a clear expectation of what they'll get from your content.

❖ Ask a question: Questions can pique your audience's curiosity and motivate them to learn more about the topic you're discussing.

❖ Use emotional triggers: Use words that evoke emotions like "love," "hate," "surprise," "fear," or others that resonate with your audience's needs and desires.

❖ Test different variations: Test different variations of your headline or title using A/B testing to see which one performs better.

The Importance of Visuals in Content Marketing

Visuals are essential in content marketing as they can boost engagement, retention, and conversions. Here's why visuals are crucial in content marketing:

❖ Catch the eye: Visuals can catch your audience's attention and make them stop scrolling through their feed or website.

❖ Convey emotions: Visuals can convey emotions and

messages more efficiently than words, creating a more memorable and emotional impact.

❖   Enhance retention: People remember visuals better than words, making them a powerful tool for enhancing content retention and engagement.

❖   Improve comprehension: Visuals can improve comprehension of complex ideas, data, or processes, making them more accessible to your audience.

❖   Facilitate social sharing: Visuals are more shareable than text-only content, making them more effective in promoting your brand and reaching new audiences.

How to Optimize Your Content for Search Engines

Optimizing your content for search engines can boost your visibility and traffic, generating more leads and conversions for your business. Here are some tips for optimizing your content for search engines:

❖   Conduct keyword research: Use keyword research tools like Google Keyword Planner or Moz Keyword Explorer to find relevant keywords and phrases related to your content topic.

❖   Optimize your headlines and titles: Use your target keywords in your headline or title to signal to search engines what your content is about.

❖   Optimize your meta description: Your meta description should provide a concise and compelling summary of your content, using your target keywords.

❖   Use alt tags for images and videos: Alt tags can provide context for search engines regarding your visuals' content, helping them understand your content better.

❖ Use internal links: Linking to other content on your website can help search engines understand your content better and improve your ranking.

❖ Use external links: Linking to authoritative sources can signal to search engines that your content is credible and trustworthy.

❖ Use structured data: structured data can make your content more accessible and relevant to search engines, improving your ranking and visibility.

In conclusion, creating compelling content is a cornerstone of any successful content marketing strategy. By focusing on providing value, engaging with your target audience, and optimizing your content for search engines, you can create content that resonates, converts, and drives your business forward.

CHAPTER 5: DISTRIBUTING YOUR CONTENT

Now that you have created compelling content, it's time to get it in front of your target audience. This is where content distribution comes in. Content distribution refers to the process of delivering your content to your audience through various channels. While creating high-quality content is important, it's equally important to ensure that it is distributed effectively. In this chapter, we will discuss different channels for content distribution and how to choose the right ones for your business.

Importance of Content Distribution

Content distribution is important because it allows you to reach a wider audience. Simply having great content is not enough. You need to get it in front of the people who would find it valuable. Not everyone will find your website or blog on their own. By distributing your content through different channels, such as social media or email marketing, you can increase your reach and attract more visitors to your website.

Different Channels for Content Distribution

There are various channels for content distribution, and each has its own advantages and disadvantages. Let's take a look at some of the most common channels:

❖ Social Media: Social media platforms are great for content distribution because they have large audiences and allow you to target specific demographics. Facebook, Twitter, LinkedIn, and Instagram are some of the most popular social media platforms for content distribution. Each platform has its own strengths and weaknesses, and it's important to choose the right platforms based on your target audience.

❖ Email Marketing: Email marketing is an effective way to distribute your content to your subscribers. It's a direct channel that allows you to communicate with your audience on a regular basis. With email marketing, you can target specific segments of your audience and personalize your messages based on their interests.

❖ Paid Advertising: Paid advertising can increase your reach and introduce your content to new audiences. Google Ads and Facebook Ads are two popular options for paid advertising. With paid advertising, you can target specific demographics and measure the effectiveness of your campaigns.

❖ Influencer Marketing: Influencer marketing involves working with influencers in your industry to promote your content. Influencers have large followings and can help you reach new audiences. It's important to choose influencers who are relevant to your industry and have a following that aligns with your target audience.

How to Choose the Right Content Distribution Channels

To choose the right content distribution channels for your business, consider the following factors:

❖ Target Audience: Who is your target audience, and where

do they spend their time online? Choose channels that align with your audience's preferences.

❖   Type of Content: Different types of content perform better on different channels. For example, visual content performs well on Instagram, while LinkedIn is better for professional content.

❖   Goals: What are your content marketing goals, and which channels will help you achieve them? If you want to increase brand awareness, social media may be the best channel for you. If you want to generate leads, email marketing or paid advertising may be more effective.

Amplifying Your Content Reach

Simply posting your content on various channels is not enough. You need to ensure that it reaches as many people as possible. Here are some tips for amplifying your content reach:

➢   Promote Your Content: Share your content on all of your social media channels and email newsletters. You can also promote your content through paid advertising.

➢   Engage with Your Audience: Respond to comments and questions on social media and email. Engaging with your audience helps build relationships and encourages social sharing.

➢   Leverage Social Shares: Encourage your audience to share your content on social media. You can also include social sharing buttons on your website and blog.

➢   Repurpose Your Content: Repurpose your content into different formats, such as videos or podcasts, to reach a wider audience.

The Role of Email Marketing in Content Distribution

Email marketing is an effective channel for content distribution because it allows you to communicate directly with your audience. Here are some tips for using email marketing to distribute your content:

❖ Segment Your Audience: Divide your email list into different segments based on interests or behaviours. This allows you to send personalized messages to each segment.

❖ Use a Catchy Subject Line: Your subject line is the first thing your audience sees in their inbox. Make it catchy and relevant to the content of your email.

❖ Include a Call-to-Action: Encourage your audience to take action by including a call-to-action in your email. This could be to read your latest blog post or watch your latest video.

❖ Measure Your Metrics: Track your email metrics, such as open rates and click-through rates, to optimize your email marketing strategy.

The Role of Influencer Marketing in Content Distribution

Influencer marketing involves working with influencers in your industry to promote your content. Here are some tips for using influencer marketing to distribute your content:

❖ Choose Relevant Influencers: Choose influencers who are relevant to your industry and have a large following. This ensures that your content reaches a wider audience.

❖ Create Valuable Content: Create high-quality content that provides value to your audience and aligns with the influencer's brand.

❖ Collaborate with Influencers: Work with influencers to create content, such as guest blog posts or social media posts, which promotes your brand.

❖ Measure Your Metrics: Track your influencer marketing metrics, such as reach and engagement, to measure the effectiveness of your campaigns.

Conclusion

Content distribution is essential for the success of your content marketing strategy. By choosing the right channels and amplifying your content reach, you can attract a wider audience and drive more traffic to your website. Email marketing and influencer marketing can be effective channels for content distribution, but it's important to choose the right channels based on your target audience and content marketing goals.

CHAPTER 6: MEASURING YOUR CONTENT PERFORMANCE

As the saying goes, "If it can't be measured, it can't be managed." In content marketing, measuring content performance is crucial to determine the effectiveness of your content strategy and make data-driven decisions to continuously improve it. In this chapter, we'll dive into the importance of measuring content performance, key metrics to track, how to analyse your data, and tips for optimizing your content strategy.

Importance of Measuring Content Performance

Measuring content performance allows you to evaluate the success of your content marketing efforts, identify areas of improvement, and optimize your strategy for better results. Without measuring your content performance, you'll have no way of knowing whether your efforts are paying off or not. Additionally, measuring your content performance helps you set realistic and achievable goals and prioritize content that resonates well with your audience.

Key Metrics to Track in Content Marketing

While there are dozens of content marketing metrics you can track, some are more important than others. Here are some of the key metrics you should track to measure your content performance:

➤ Traffic: The number of visitors to your website and landing pages is a crucial metric to track. Traffic indicates how well your content is attracting your target audience and can help you identify which channels are driving the most traffic.

➤ Engagement: Engagement metrics, such as likes, comments, shares, and time spent on page, indicate how well your content resonates with your audience and how engaged they are with it.

➤ Conversions: Conversions are the most significant metric in content marketing as they indicate whether your content is attracting the right visitors and driving them to take action. Conversion metrics include form submissions, downloads, sign-ups, and purchases.

➤ Social Media Metrics: Social media metrics, such as reach, engagement, clicks, and shares, indicate how well your content is performing on social media channels. Social media metrics can help you identify which types and formats of content work best for each platform.

➤ SEO Metrics: SEO metrics, such as rankings, organic traffic, and backlinks, indicate how well your content ranks on search engines and how visible it is to your target audience.

➤ Email Marketing Metrics: Email marketing metrics, such as open rate, click-through rate, and unsubscribe rate, indicate how well your email content performs and how engaged your email list is.

How to Create a Content Performance Dashboard

To effectively measure your content marketing performance, it's best to create a dashboard that tracks all your key metrics in one place. A content performance dashboard is a visual representation of your content marketing data that shows trends, patterns, and insights.

When creating a content performance dashboard, consider the following:

➢ Choose the right metrics: Select the key metrics that are relevant to your content marketing goals and objectives.

➢ Choose the right tools: Choose the right analytics tools that allow you to track and measure your data.

➢ Decide on the frequency of reporting: Decide how often you'll analyse and report your data and update your dashboard accordingly.

➢ Visualize your data: Use charts, graphs, and other visual elements to create a user-friendly and informative dashboard.

How to Analyse Your Content Metrics

Analysing your content metrics involves interpreting your data to identify trends, opportunities, and areas for improvement. Here are some tips for analysing your content metrics:

❖ Look for patterns and trends: Identify patterns in your data over time and look for trends that indicate what is working well and what needs improvement.

❖ Segment your data: Segment your data by content type, channel, audience, and other relevant factors to uncover insights and identify areas for improvement.

❖ Measure performance against goals: Measure your performance against your content marketing goals and objectives to determine whether you're on track.

❖ Compare your data: Compare your data against industry benchmarks and your competitors to see how you're performing.

How to Use Data to Optimize Your Content Strategy

Using data to optimize your content strategy involves using your insights to make data-driven decisions that improve your content marketing performance. Here are some tips for using data to optimize your content strategy:

❖ Focus on what works: Use your data to identify and prioritize content types, channels, and formats that have proven successful in the past.

❖ Experiment and test: Use A/B testing and experimentation to try out new content ideas and measure their effectiveness.

❖ Optimize your content for SEO: Use your SEO data to optimize your website content for better search engine rankings and visibility.

❖ Optimize your content for engagement: Use your engagement data to optimize your content for better engagement and interaction with your audience.

❖ Stay flexible: Be prepared to change your content strategy based on your data insights and adapt to new trends and best practices.

Tips for Experimenting and Testing Your Content

Experimenting and testing your content is a key part of using data to optimize your content strategy. Here are some tips for experimenting and testing your content:

❖ Set clear goals: Set clear goals for your experiments, such as increasing traffic, engagement, or conversions.

❖ Test one variable at a time: Test one variable at a time, such as the headline, the call-to-action, or the content format, to see what works best.

❖ Measure your data: Measure your data before and after the experiment to determine whether it was successful.

❖ Document your results: Document your results and insights to use in future content campaigns.

How to Continuously Improve Your Content Performance

Continuous improvement is a critical aspect of content marketing success. Here are some tips for continuously improving your content performance:

❖ Consistently analyse your data: Regularly analyse your data to identify what's working and what's not.

❖ Stay up-to-date on trends and best practices: Stay up-to-date on the latest content marketing trends and best practices to stay relevant and competitive.

❖ Attend industry events: Attend industry events and conferences to learn from experts and network with peers.

❖ Listen to feedback: Listen to feedback from your audience and use it to improve your content.

❖ Work with a team: Work with a team of content marketing professionals who can provide fresh ideas and perspectives for improvement.

Summary

Measuring your content performance is essential to determine the effectiveness of your content marketing strategy. Key metrics to track include traffic, engagement, conversions, social media metrics, SEO metrics, and email marketing metrics. Creating a content performance dashboard, analysing your data, using data to optimize your content strategy, and experimenting and testing your content are all critical steps to continuously improve your content performance over time.

CHAPTER 7: REPURPOSING YOUR CONTENT

Content creation can eat up a lot of time and resources, which is why repurposing your content is an excellent strategy to maximize its value and reach. Repurposing your content means taking existing content and transforming it into something new, fresh, and relevant to your target audience. In this chapter, we'll discuss the importance of repurposing your content and explore different ways to repurpose your content.

Importance of Repurposing Content

Repurposing content can benefit your content marketing strategy in several ways. Firstly, it helps to increase the lifespan of your content. For instance, a blog post that was published months or years ago can be transformed into an ebook, video, or podcast, allowing you to reach a new audience.

Secondly, it saves time and resources. When you have created content that resonates with your audience, repurposing it allows you to leverage that content to create more valuable and informative pieces.

Thirdly, repurposing content can help improve your search engine optimization (SEO) efforts. When you repurpose a piece of content, you can use relevant keywords and phrases, which can boost your visibility and improve your search engine ranking.

Different Ways to Repurpose Content

1. Turn a Blog Post into an Ebook

Turning a blog post into an ebook is one of the most effective ways to repurpose content. An ebook allows you to go deeper into a topic and provide your audience with a comprehensive guide. You can leverage your existing blog content to create an ebook, and this can be shared on your website or downloaded by your audience.

2. Repurpose Blog Posts into Infographics

A blog post can be repurposed into an infographic. Infographics are highly visual, and they make it easy for your audience to consume information quickly. Add visual and graphic elements, such as charts, graphs, and images, to help reinforce the main points and make the content more visually appealing.

3. Transform a Blog Post into a Podcast

Repurposing a blog post into a podcast allows you to deliver the same information in a new format. Podcasts are becoming increasingly popular, and they offer an opportunity to reach a new audience. Create a script from your blog post and use it as a guide when recording your podcast episode.

4. Repurpose Case Studies into Videos

Case studies are powerful tools that can help build trust with your audience. Transforming them into videos can make them more compelling and engaging. You can use animations, interviews, or customer testimonials to bring your case study to life.

5. Turn Social Media Posts into Blog Posts

If you've been creating social media posts that have been generating engagement from your audience, repurpose them into blog posts. Collate a few of the related posts, add some insights, and expand on the points that you made on social media.

6. Use Data-Driven Stories for Multiple Channels

If you've conducted research and have data to share, you can use this data to create multiple pieces of content. Data-driven stories can be turned into blog posts, infographics, and social media posts. You can even pitch them to journalists to create a media story.

How to Identify Content That Can Be Repurposed

Not every piece of content can be repurposed, but some types of content lend themselves well to repurposing. Here are some ways to identify content that can be repurposed:

1. Identify Evergreen Content

Look at your analytics to see which pieces of content have generated the most traffic and engagement. Evergreen content tends to be timeless, and it's the type of content that people continue to search for months or years after it's been published. This type of content can be repurposed into various formats and shared with your audience again.

2. Spot Trends in Your Industry

Look at the trending topics in your industry. If there's a topic that's generating a lot of buzz, you can repurpose your existing content on that topic to share with your audience.

3. Review Seasonal Content

If you have seasonal content, such as holiday-themed blog posts, you can update and repurpose them year after year. For example, a Christmas-themed blog post can be updated with new statistics and trends every year and repurposed into an ebook, podcast, or infographic.

4. Leverage User-Generated Content

If your audience or customers are sharing stories or reviews about your product or service, you can repurpose these into blog posts, social media posts, or even customer testimonials.

How to Repurpose Content for Different Channels

Repurposing content can involve taking a piece of content and using it across multiple channels. Here are some ways to repurpose content for different channels:

1. Use Visuals

Visuals, such as images, infographics, and videos, are essential elements in content marketing. Using visuals can help you repurpose your content for different channels, as they can be used across social media platforms, email marketing campaigns, and ebooks.

2. Look for Ways to Slice and Dice Content

A single piece of content, such as an ebook or white paper, can be sliced and diced to create different formats that cater to different audiences. An ebook, for instance, can be repurposed into a series of blog posts or social media posts.

3. Use Social Media to Amplify Your Content Reach

Social media platforms, such as Facebook, Twitter, and LinkedIn, offer an excellent opportunity to repurpose content. You can share links to blog posts, infographics, and videos on social media to reach a broader audience.

4. Tailor Content for Different Platforms

Different channels have various requirements, and what works for one platform may not work for another. It's essential to tailor your content for different platforms to ensure that it's effective. For example, a video intended for YouTube may need to be shorter than one intended for LinkedIn.

How to Update and Refresh Your Old Content

Repurposing content doesn't necessarily mean creating new content from scratch. Sometimes, updating and refreshing old content can be just as effective. Here are some ways to update old content:

1. Add New Information

Adding new information to an old blog post can give it a new lease on life. Review older blog posts to see if there are any new statistics, trends, or insights that you can add.

2. Update Images and Visuals

Updating images and visuals in an old blog post can freshen it up and make it more visually appealing. Replace outdated images with updated ones that align with your brand's image.

3. Optimize for Search Engines

Review your old content to see if it's optimized for search engines. Updating old content to include relevant keywords and meta descriptions can improve its visibility and drive traffic to your website.

4. Change the Format

Converting your old content into a different format can give it a new lease on life. For instance, a blog post published last year can be repurposed into a podcast episode or an infographic.

The Benefits of Repurposing Content for SEO

Repurposing content can benefit your SEO efforts in several ways. Firstly, repurposing content helps improve your website's user experience by providing various content formats to suit different audiences. Search engines value quality user experience and, hence, sites which offer a variety of content formats rank higher.

Secondly, repurposing content can help boost your site's search engine ranking by widening its reach. When you repurpose your content, you have an opportunity to use new keywords and increase interlinking, which helps your site to rank higher in search engine results pages.

Lastly, repurposing content can help you save time and money by creating multiple pieces of content from a single piece of content.

How to Create a Repurposing Strategy

Creating a repurposing strategy can help you leverage your existing content to its full potential. Here are the steps to creating a repurposing strategy:

1. Identify Your Goals

The first step in creating a repurposing strategy is to identify your goals. Think about why you're repurposing content and what you hope to achieve. Do you want to reach a wider audience? Are you looking to improve your SEO efforts? Identifying your goal will help you determine the type of content to repurpose.

2. Audit Your Existing Content

Conduct an audit of your existing content to determine what content to repurpose. Look through your blogs, social media posts, and other content to find pieces that have resonated with your audience or have performed well. Also, identify content that can be updated or repurposed to meet your current goals.

3. Choose Your Formats

The next step is to determine the formats to repurpose your content. Choose formats that suit both your audience's preferences and the content you've identified. For instance, if you want to target millennials, consider repurposing your content into videos or social media posts.

4. Create a Repurposing Schedule

Creating a repurposing schedule can help you make the most out of your content and ensure that you're consistently producing content that resonates with your audience. Determine how often you want to repurpose content and develop a schedule that aligns with your other content marketing efforts.

5. Measure Your Success

Measuring the success of your repurposing strategy is essential to determine if it's been effective. Track metrics such as website traffic, engagement levels, and conversion rates to determine how successful your repurposed content has been in achieving your goals.

Summary

Repurposing content is a valuable strategy that can help you save time and resources while reaching a broader audience. To leverage the benefits of repurposing content, you need to identify content that can be repurposed, determine the appropriate formats, and establish a repurposing schedule. Remember to measure the success of your repurposing efforts to determine if it's aligning with your content marketing goals.

CHAPTER 8: BUILDING A SUCCESSFUL BLOG

Blogging has been around for over two decades, yet it remains a crucial aspect of content marketing. Blogs have evolved from being a platform for people to share their personal thoughts and experiences to becoming a valuable tool for businesses in creating brand awareness, building trust with customers, and driving traffic to their website. In this chapter, we'll dive into the importance of blogging, how to get started, how to create engaging posts, and how to optimize your blog for search engines.

Importance of Blogging for Content Marketing

At its core, blogging is about sharing information that will provide value to your target audience. By creating and sharing high-quality content on a consistent basis, you can establish yourself as a thought leader in your industry, build a community of followers, and attract new customers to your business.

Blogging also plays a significant role in Search Engine Optimization (SEO). Google and other search engines love fresh, relevant content, and by regularly publishing new blog posts, you increase your chances of ranking higher in search engine results pages (SERPs). This can, in turn, drive more traffic to your website and ultimately lead to more conversions.

How to Start a Blog

Starting a blog is relatively easy, and there are several platforms available, including WordPress, Squarespace, and Blogger. However, before you dive in, it's important to have a clear understanding of your blog's purpose and who your target audience is.

Once you have defined your blog's purpose and audience, you'll want to choose a domain name and hosting service. Your domain name should be unique, memorable, and reflect your brand's personality. Your hosting service should be reliable, secure, and offer features that meet your blogging needs.

After setting up your blog, you'll want to customize its appearance to reflect your brand's identity. This can include choosing a theme, adding a logo, and creating a consistent colour scheme across your blog.

Tips for Creating Engaging Blog Posts

Your blog posts should be informative, engaging, and written in a conversational tone. Here are some tips to keep in mind when creating content for your blog:

➢ Know your audience: Understanding your target audience is critical to creating content that resonates with them. Use the audience research tactics discussed in Chapter 2 to identify their pain points, needs, and preferences.

➢ Choose relevant topics: Focus on topics that are relevant to your audience and aligned with your overall content strategy. Use keyword research to find popular topics in your industry that haven't been covered extensively.

➢ Write compelling headlines: Your headlines should be attention-grabbing and accurately reflect the content of your post. Use numbers, questions, and power words to make your headlines more compelling.

➤ Use storytelling: Incorporate storytelling in your blog posts to make them more relatable and engaging. Humans are wired to respond to stories emotionally, so weave personal experiences or customer success stories into your writing.

➤ Use visuals: Including images, infographics, and videos in your blog posts can make them more visually appealing and easy to digest.

➤ Use formatting: Break up long paragraphs with headers, bulleted lists, and numbered lists to make your content more readable.

➤ End with a call to action: Every blog post should have a clear call to action that prompts the reader to take action. This can be an invitation to subscribe to your newsletter, download a free resource, or schedule a consultation.

How to Optimize Your Blog for Search Engines

Creating high-quality content is just one aspect of optimizing your blog for search engines. Here are some additional tips for improving your blog's visibility in SERPs:

❖ Use keywords: Use keywords strategically in your blog posts, including in the headline, meta description, and throughout the body. However, avoid keyword stuffing and ensure that your content flows naturally.

❖ Use metadata: Meta tags, including the title tag and meta description, provide context to search engines about the content of your blog post. An accurate and relevant title tag and meta description can improve click-through rates from organic search results.

❖ Use internal linking: Consistently link to other blog posts and pages on your website when relevant. This helps search engines understand the relationship between different pieces of content on your site.

❖ Use external linking: Link to authoritative sources when relevant. This can improve the credibility of your content and demonstrate your expertise on the subject matter.

❖ Make your blog mobile-responsive: With more and more people accessing the internet on mobile devices, it's essential to ensure that your blog is optimized for smaller screens.

❖ Monitor your analytics: Monitor your blog's traffic and engagement metrics regularly to gauge the effectiveness of your content and adjust your strategy accordingly.

Conclusion

Blogging remains a valuable tool in any content marketing strategy. By focusing on your audience's needs, creating high-quality content, and optimizing your blog for search engines, you can establish yourself as a thought leader in your industry and attract new customers to your business. Remember to stay consistent and persistent in your blogging efforts, and you'll reap the benefits over time.

CHAPTER 9: CREATING EFFECTIVE VIDEO CONTENT

In the world of content marketing, video is one of the most powerful tools available to businesses. The popularity of online video continues to soar, making it a must-have for any business looking to engage with its audience and ultimately drive conversions. In this chapter, we will explore the best practices and strategies for creating effective video content that resonates with your target audience.

Importance of Video Content

There are several reasons why video content has become such an essential part of a successful content marketing strategy.

First, video is highly engaging. It is a highly visual medium, and it is a great way to convey complex ideas and information in an easy-to-understand format. Video also allows businesses to showcase their products or services in a way that is both entertaining and informative.

Second, video content is easily shareable. People love to share videos they find interesting, funny or informative, and social media platforms make it easy for video content to go viral. This means that businesses can reach a wider audience much faster than with other forms of content.

Third, video content is highly versatile. It can be used in a variety of ways, from product demos to brand storytelling to customer testimonials. This means that businesses can create a wide range of video content that caters to different stages of the customer journey.

Different Types of Video Content

There are many different types of video content that businesses can create, depending on their marketing goals and the preferences of their target audience. Here are some of the most common types of video content:

❖ Brand videos: These videos are designed to introduce your brand to your target audience. They are typically short, visually captivating and include a strong call-to-action (CTA) at the end.

❖ Explainer videos: These videos are designed to explain complex topics or ideas in an easy-to-understand format. They are often animated and use simple visuals to keep the viewer engaged.

❖ Product demo videos: These videos showcase your products or services in action. They can be used to highlight the key features and benefits of your offerings and are a great way to showcase the value you provide to your customers.

❖ Customer testimonials: These videos feature happy customers sharing their positive experiences with your product or service. They are a powerful tool for building trust and credibility with your target audience.

❖ How-to videos: These videos explain how to use your product or service. They are a great resource for customers who need help getting started and can be a powerful tool for driving conversions.

Planning and Scripting Your Videos

The key to creating effective video content is careful planning and scripting. Before you start filming, it is important to define your goals and determine the type of video you want to create. Here are some steps to follow:

Step 1: Define your goals: What do you want to achieve with your video? Do you want to increase brand awareness, drive traffic to your website, or generate leads? Defining your goals will help you determine the type of video you want to create and the key message you want to convey.

Step 2: Identify your target audience: Who is your video designed for? What are their pain points and challenges? Understanding your audience will help you create a video that resonates with them and addresses their needs.

Step 3: Develop your key message: What is the one key message you want your audience to remember after watching your video? Keep it simple and focused on the benefits your product or service provides.

Step 4: Storyboard your video: A storyboard is a visual representation of your video. It outlines the scenes, shots and dialogue for each part of your video. This helps you visualize your video and ensure that it flows smoothly.

Step 5: Write a script: Your script should be concise, engaging and easy to follow. Use persuasive language to highlight the benefits of your product or service and keep your audience engaged throughout.

Tips for Filming and Editing Your Videos

Once you have your script in place, it's time to start filming. Here are some tips to help you create high-quality video content:

❖ Start with high-quality equipment: While you don't need to break the bank on equipment, you do need to make sure that your video is clear, and the sound is easy to hear. Invest in a good camera and microphone to ensure that your video looks and sounds great.

❖ Use good lighting: Lighting is key to creating a high-quality video. Make sure you film in a well-lit area, and avoid filming in direct sunlight or areas with harsh shadows.

❖ Keep it short and sweet: Most online viewers have short attention spans, so it pays to keep your videos short and to the point. Aim for videos that are two to three minutes in length, and cut out any unnecessary content.

❖ Use engaging visuals: Your video should be visually captivating to keep your audience engaged. Use a mix of shots and angles to keep your video visually interesting.

❖ Add music: Adding music to your video can help set the tone and add emotional resonance to your message. Just make sure the music doesn't distract from your message.

Optimizing Your Video for Search Engines

Once your video is live, it's important to optimize it for search engines. Here are some tips to help you get your video seen:

➢ Use keywords: Just like with written content, it's important to use keywords in your video file names, titles and descriptions. This helps search engines understand what your video is about and improves your chances of ranking in search results.

➢ Add a transcript: Transcribing your video helps make it more accessible and also provides more content for search engines to crawl.

➢ Promote your video: Share your video across all your social media channels, embed it on your website and include it in your email campaigns. The more exposure your video gets, the greater its chances of being seen by your target audience.

The Importance of Video Analytics

Finally, it's important to track the performance of your video using analytics. Here are some metrics to track:

- ❖ Views: This metric measures how many people have viewed your video.

- ❖ Engagement: This metric measures how long people are watching your video and whether they are engaging with it in other ways, such as by liking or sharing it.

- ❖ Conversions: This metric measures how many people took action after watching your video, such as by visiting your website or making a purchase.

By tracking video analytics, you can identify what is working well and what needs improvement. Use this data to continuously improve your video content and ensure that it remains effective over time.

In conclusion, video content is a vital part of any successful content marketing strategy. By following these best practices and strategies for creating effective video content, you can engage with your target audience, build trust and credibility, and ultimately drive conversions.

CHAPTER 10: DEVELOPING A THOUGHT LEADERSHIP STRATEGY

If you want to establish your business as a thought leader in your industry, getting your content marketing right is essential. Thought leadership is all about being perceived as an expert in your field, and businesses that are seen as thought leaders can enjoy a wealth of benefits. These include attracting top talent, earning media coverage, building brand trust, and ultimately increasing sales.

But how do you develop a thought leadership strategy that actually works? In this chapter, we will guide you through the steps you need to take to become a thought leader in your industry.

Importance of Thought Leadership in Content Marketing

In today's highly competitive market, businesses need to stand out from the crowd and demonstrate their unique value proposition. Thought leadership is a valuable tool for doing just that. By sharing your unique insights and perspectives, you can differentiate your business from your competitors and gain the trust of potential customers. Essentially, thought leadership helps you to establish your brand as a reputable source of information and opinion in your industry.

Different Formats for Thought Leadership Content

Thought leadership content can come in a variety of forms, including:

➢ Whitepapers: detailed reports that provide industry insights and analysis

➢ Blogs: regular insights, opinions, and perspectives shared on a company blog

➢ Webinars: online seminars that offer new insights and perspectives on a particular topic

➢ Podcasts: audio content that offers unique perspectives on industry trends and news

➢ Social media: regular sharing of valuable insights on LinkedIn, Twitter or other social media platforms

➢ Speaking engagements: attending industry events and speaking at conferences

Tips for Creating Thought Leadership Content

Creating thought leadership content that stands out from the crowd can be a daunting task. Here are some tips to help you develop content that positions you as an expert in your industry.

1. Focus on Providing Value

When creating thought leadership content, focus on providing value to your target audience. Your content should offer insights, ideas, or opinions that your audience can't find anywhere else.

Remember, your content should educate and inform rather than simply selling your products or services.

2. Be Authentic

Authenticity is key when it comes to creating thought leadership content. Share your personal experiences, challenges and opinions about industry trends. The more authentic you are, the more likely people will connect with you and your content.

3. Offer Actionable Insights

To position your business as a thought leader, your content should offer actionable insights that your audience can use in their own businesses. You want your content to be practical, relevant and applicable to the needs of your target audience.

4. Use Data to Support Your Arguments

Using data to support your arguments can help to establish your business as a reputable source of information in your industry. Incorporate statistics or surveys that support your insights and help your audience to understand trends or issues more clearly.

5. Experiment with Different Formats

Experimenting with different content formats can help you to find the type of content that resonates most with your target audience. Try creating blog posts, webinars or podcasts to see which format gets the most traction.

How to Promote Your Thought Leadership Content

Creating thought leadership content is just the first step - you also need to promote it effectively. Here are some tips for promoting your content:

1. Use Social Media

Social media can be a powerful tool for promoting your thought leadership content. Share your content on LinkedIn, Twitter, and other social media platforms, and engage with your audience to build a following.

2. Leverage Influencers

Influencers in your industry can help to amplify your content. Connect with influencers on social media and share your content with them, asking for their feedback and asking them to share it with their own followers.

3. Attend Industry Events

Speaking at industry events can also help you to promote your thought leadership content. Use the event to showcase your expertise and connect with others in your industry.

4. Incorporate SEO

Incorporating search engine optimization (SEO) techniques into your content can help to improve its visibility. Use relevant keywords and phrases, create meta descriptions, and link back to other pages on your website to boost your search engine rankings.

5. Engage with Your Audience

Engage with your audience to build a relationship of trust and respect. Respond to comments, answer questions and show that you value their feedback.

The Benefits of Being a Thought Leader

The benefits of being perceived as a thought leader in your

industry are numerous. By creating thought leadership content that offers unique insights and perspectives, you can set your business apart from your competitors and become the go-to source for information in your industry. This can lead to increased brand exposure, higher lead generation and overall, help to establish your business as a reputable and trusted authority.

Summary

Thought leadership is a powerful tool for establishing your business as an industry expert. By creating valuable content that offers unique insights and perspectives, you can differentiate yourself from your competitors and build a loyal following. To create thought leadership content that resonates with your target audience, focus on providing value, being authentic, offering actionable insights, using data to support your arguments, and experimenting with different content formats. To promote your content, utilize social media, leverage influencers, attend industry events, incorporate SEO best practices, and engage with your audience. Overall, becoming a thought leader can help to boost your business's brand exposure, lead generation, and ultimately, increase your bottom line.

CHAPTER 11: UTILIZING USER-GENERATED CONTENT

When it comes to content marketing, user-generated content (UGC) can be an incredibly powerful resource for businesses. User-generated content includes any content that is created by customers or fans of a brand, such as reviews, testimonials, photos, and social media posts. By harnessing the power of user-generated content, businesses can increase brand awareness, build trust and loyalty with their audience, and drive conversions.

Importance of User-Generated Content

Consumers are more likely to trust user-generated content over branded content because it is created by real people with real experiences. In fact, according to a recent survey, 90% of consumers say that UGC has more influence over their purchasing decisions than any other type of content.

In addition, user-generated content can help businesses create a sense of community around their brand. When customers see that other people are engaging with and supporting the brand, they are more likely to feel a sense of connection and loyalty to the brand themselves.

Different Types of User-Generated Content

There are many different types of user-generated content that businesses can leverage, including:

❖ Reviews and Testimonials: Reviews and testimonials from happy customers can be incredibly persuasive in convincing potential customers to try a product or service. Brands can feature customer reviews on their website or social media channels to showcase their social proof and build trust with their audience.

❖ Photos and Videos: Visual content created by customers can be used to showcase the experiences and benefits of a product or service. Brands can encourage customers to share their photos on social media using a branded hashtag or by hosting a photo contest.

❖ Social Media Posts: Social media posts created by customers can be a valuable source of user-generated content. Brands can share user-generated content on their own social media channels to show their appreciation for their customers and build a stronger relationship with their audience.

How to Encourage User-Generated Content

Encouraging customers to create and share user-generated content can be a great way to build a stronger relationship with your audience and expand your reach. Here are some tips for encouraging user-generated content:

❖ Offer Incentives: One effective way to encourage customers to share content is to offer incentives such as discounts or prizes for the best user-generated content.

❖ Create a Hashtag Campaign: Creating a branded hashtag campaign can encourage customers to share their experiences with your brand on social media. Make sure to choose a catchy and easy to remember hashtag that fits with your brand messaging.

❖ Develop Shareable Content: Creating shareable content that is entertaining or informative can encourage customers to share it with their own followers. This could include creating how-to guides, infographics, or funny memes related to your brand.

How to Curate User-Generated Content

Once you have collected user-generated content, it's important to curate and feature it in a way that is engaging for your audience. Here are some tips for curating user-generated content:

❖ Choose High-Quality Content: Make sure to choose user-generated content that is high-quality and showcases your brand in a positive light.

❖ Give Credit: Always make sure to give credit to the customers who created the content by tagging them in social media posts or featuring their name in testimonials.

❖ Showcase Variety: Don't be afraid to showcase a variety of user-generated content types to keep things interesting for your audience. This could include featuring different customers each week or highlighting a range of products or services.

How to Use User-Generated Content in Your Marketing Campaigns

Now that you have collected and curated user-generated content, it's time to put it to work in your marketing campaigns. Here are some tips for using user-generated content effectively:

❖ Incorporate UGC into Your Website: Consider featuring customer reviews and testimonials prominently on your website to showcase your social proof.

❖ Share on Social Media: Share user-generated content on

your social media channels to engage with your audience and show appreciation for your customers.

❖   Use in Advertising: Incorporate user-generated content into your advertising campaigns to add an element of authenticity and build trust with potential customers.

Tips for Managing User-Generated Content

Managing user-generated content effectively is essential to maintaining a positive brand image and avoiding any legal or reputation issues. Here are some tips for managing user-generated content:

❖   Set Guidelines: Create clear guidelines for what types of content are acceptable for user-generated content campaigns and how you will feature that content.

❖   Monitor for Inappropriate Content: Regularly monitor user-generated content to ensure that it meets your brand standards and doesn't include any inappropriate or offensive content.

❖   Respond to Negative Feedback: Be prepared to respond to negative feedback or reviews in a timely and professional manner to show that you value customer feedback and are committed to addressing any issues.

Conclusion

User-generated content can be a highly effective tool for building trust, engagement, and loyalty with your audience. By encouraging customers to share their experiences with your brand, you can create a sense of community and showcase your social proof to potential customers. To get the most out of user-generated content, it's important to curate it effectively, use it strategically in your marketing campaigns, and manage it carefully to protect your brand image and reputation.

CHAPTER 12: LEVERAGING SOCIAL MEDIA FOR CONTENT MARKETING

In today's digital age, social media has become the go-to platform for businesses to engage with their customers. With over 3.6 billion active users worldwide, social media presents a unique opportunity for businesses to connect with their target audience, build brand awareness, and ultimately drive sales. Social media can be an extremely powerful tool for content marketing, if used effectively. In this chapter, we'll look at how you can use social media to promote your content and engage with your audience.

Different Social Media Platforms for Content Marketing

There are numerous social media platforms available today, each with its strengths and benefits. The most popular social media platforms for content marketing include Facebook, Twitter, LinkedIn, Instagram, and Pinterest.

➤ Facebook: With over 2.8 billion monthly active users, Facebook is the largest social media platform globally and the ideal place to reach a wide audience. Facebook is a platform that encourages content sharing, so businesses can leverage users' interest to engage with their content.

> ➤ Twitter: Twitter is a fast-paced social media platform where businesses can share their content in short, engaging messages. With over 330 million monthly active users, Twitter can be a great platform for brands to increase their visibility and engage with their audience.

> ➤ LinkedIn: As a professional networking platform, LinkedIn is the best place to connect with potential customers, partners, and employees. With over 722 million members worldwide, LinkedIn represents a great opportunity for businesses to share thought leadership content and position themselves as industry leaders.

> ➤ Instagram: With over 1 billion monthly active users, Instagram is the most popular social media platform for visual content. Instagram is a highly engaging platform where businesses can share images, videos, and Stories to engage with their audience.

> ➤ Pinterest: Pinterest is a visual discovery engine where users can discover new ideas, products, and tips. With over 440 million monthly active users, Pinterest represents a unique opportunity for businesses to share their product images, videos, and other visually appealing content.

How to Create Engaging Social Media Posts

To create engaging social media posts, you need to keep your audience in mind. Here are some tips to create engaging social media posts:

> ❖ Use visual content: Visual content like images, videos, and infographics can grab users' attention and encourage engagement. Make sure your visuals are high-quality and optimized for the platform you're using.

> ❖ Keep it short: Social media platforms have character limits, so it's best to keep your posts brief and to the point.

Use concise and powerful language to grab your audience's attention.

❖ Use relevant hashtags: Hashtags help users discover content on social media platforms. Use relevant hashtags to increase the visibility of your posts and reach a wider audience.

❖ Ask questions: Asking questions in your posts is a great way to engage with your audience and prompt a conversation. Make sure your questions are relevant to your audience and your content.

❖ Run contests: Running social media contests and giveaways is an excellent way to boost engagement and drive traffic to your website.

How to Optimize Your Social Media Profiles

Optimizing your social media profiles is essential to ensure your content is seen by your target audience. Here's how you can optimize your social media profiles:

➢ Use a consistent profile picture: Use the same profile picture across all your social media profiles to ensure consistency. Your profile picture should be recognizable and represent your brand.

➢ Use a clear and concise bio: Your bio should briefly describe your brand and what you do. It should also include relevant keywords that represent your business.

➢ Use relevant keywords: Using relevant keywords in your social media profiles will help your business appear in search results.

➢ Provide your contact information: Make sure your contact information, like your email, phone number, and website, are easily accessible on your social media profiles.

How to Use Social Media Advertising in Your Content Marketing

Incorporating social media advertising into your content marketing strategy can help increase your reach and engagement. Here are some tips for using social media advertising:

❖ Set clear goals: Before you begin your social media advertising, set clear goals and objectives. Are you looking to increase brand awareness or drive sales?

❖ Choose the right platform: Choose the social media platform that aligns with your advertising goals. Each platform has different advertising options, targeting, and costs.

❖ Use high-quality visuals: Use high-quality images and videos to grab users' attention and encourage engagement.

❖ Target your ads effectively: Target your ads using the right demographics, behaviours, interests, and location.

❖ Test and experiment: Test and experiment with different ad formats, visuals, and copy to see what works best for your business.

How to Track and Analyse Your Social Media Metrics

To ensure your social media efforts are effective, you need to track and analyse your social media metrics. Some key metrics to track include engagement rate, follower growth rate, click-through rate, and conversion rate. Use social media analytics tools to measure your metrics and adjust your strategy accordingly.

Tips for Building a Social Media Following

Building a social media following takes time and patience. Here are some tips for building a social media following:

➢ Create engaging content: Create content that resonates with your target audience and is shareable.

➢ Post consistently: Post regularly to keep your audience engaged and up-to-date with your brand.

➢ Engage with your audience: Respond to comments, messages, and posts to build a relationship with your audience.

➢ Use relevant hashtags: Use relevant hashtags to increase the visibility of your content and reach a wider audience.

➢ Collaborate with others: Collaborate with influencers, complementary businesses, and thought leaders to reach new audiences and build brand awareness.

Summary

Social media is a powerful tool for content marketing. With the right strategies, businesses can leverage social media platforms to reach their target audience, engage with them, and ultimately drive sales. By optimizing your social media profiles, creating engaging social media posts, using social media advertising, tracking your social media metrics, and building a social media following, you can effectively use social media to promote your content and achieve your content marketing goals.

CHAPTER 13: CREATING INTERACTIVE CONTENT

Content creation is an essential part of digital marketing, yet engaging the audience can be challenging. Static content, such as text and images, no longer suffice. Today's customers crave interactive content, something they can engage with a little more than a scroll and like a button. Interactive content has emerged as an engaging way to supply digital content and is gaining popularity fast. In this chapter, we will explore the importance of interactive content and ways to create engaging interactive content for your audience.

Importance of Interactive Content

Interactive content is a type of digital content that encourages user participation, resulting in a two-way conversation with the target audience. Interactive content could come in different formats, including quizzes, calculators, polls, surveys, infographics, games, webinars, augmented reality, virtual reality, and podcasts. It is engaging, memorable, and has several benefits that make it a vital part of digital marketing.

Interactive content is essential in generating more leads. Offering the audience a more personalized experience can help qualify leads better, resulting in better conversions. Interactive content can also help build trust with your audience. The more engaged they are, the more likely they are to improve their understanding of a product, service or brand, helping you connect better with potential customers. Interactive content is also ideal for building brand awareness, especially for start-ups or new products and services. It can be a great and more memorable way of telling your brand's stories.

Different Formats for Interactive Content

Before jumping into creating interactive content, it's essential to understand the various types of interactive content formats that your business can use to achieve its goals. Each format has its advantages and disadvantages, depending on the purpose and the target audience.

One of these formats is Interactive Infographics. Interactive Infographics provides a visual aid that helps in the easy understanding of data and complex ideas, and appeals to all senses in a more engaging and interactive manner. Interactive Infographics allow the users to interact with the data, filtering visual displays with a click, opening and revealing new information, or redirecting to a web page.

Another interactive content format is Surveys and polls. These are relatively easy to create and are an excellent way of getting feedback from your audience or target market. This form of interactive content is valuable in gathering insights and feedback on products, services or strategic content plans.

Quizzes and games create a more captivating experience and can be a fun and entertaining way to interact with customers. Games and quizzes can also go viral, amplifying your brand's reach.

Augmented reality and Virtual reality are immersive and exciting technologies for interactive content. They give users a more engaging experience and allow them to become more involved with the product or service, building on the relationship with your brand.

Creating Engaging Interactive Content

Creating compelling interactive content requires a combination of technologies, creativity, strategy and understanding your audience. Whether you're creating surveys, quizzes, infographics or games, here are some necessary steps to ensure your interactive content achieves its goals.

❖　Define Goals: To create engaging interactive content, define the goals you hope to achieve, as it guides the creation process. What results are you looking for, and why is it relevant to your target audience?

❖　Determine Your Target Audience: Identify your target audience, then develop content strategies that cater to their interests and needs. Create interactive content that appeals to its audience's demographics and psychographics.

❖　Research your Interactive Content: Research your interactive content and figure out how your audience interacts and how your interactive content fits into their online journey. How can you appeal to their interests or individualization?

❖　Plan Your Interactive Content: Using the research you've conducted, plan your interactive content. Decide on formats that work based on your audience's preferences.

❖　Design Engaging Content: Focus on designing engaging content that is compelling and interactive enough to catch the audience's attention. The content must be visually and contextually appealing to make a lasting impression.

❖　Keep It Simple: While creating interactive content,

remember to keep it simple. Avoid making the content too complex, which may lose your audience's attention.

❖ Value Proposition: Ensure that your interactive content aligns with your brand's value proposition, which is crucial to building trust with your audience.

❖ Launch, Promote, Measure, and Adjust: Launch your interactive content, promote it through the appropriate digital channels, measure its effectiveness and adjust as necessary to achieve its strategic goals.

Final Thoughts

Interactive content can be a great way to cut through the digital noise surrounding many brands' marketing efforts. The right interactive content holds a user's attention, appeals to their emotions, and provides them with engaging content that can help boost your business conversation rates. Remember to create content that is simple, visually and contextually appealing, and tries to align with your brand's value proposition. These tips and the tools available will prove valuable as you embark on your journey to creating engaging interactive content for your digital marketing strategy.

CHAPTER 14: INCORPORATING BRAND STORYTELLING

One of the most effective ways to engage an audience and build a connection with them is through storytelling. And in the context of content marketing, this translates into brand storytelling. Brand storytelling is the art of conveying a narrative about your brand that is aligned with its values, personality, and objectives. It is a powerful tool to differentiate your brand from others in the market, by creating an emotional connection with your audience that goes beyond product features or services.

In this chapter, we will delve into the importance of brand storytelling in content marketing, its different elements, how to develop a compelling brand story, and tips for integrating it across all marketing channels.

Importance of Brand Storytelling in Content Marketing

In the digital age, where consumers are bombarded with a plethora of content, it's imperative to create content that stands out and resonates with your audience. And there's no better way to achieve this than through brand storytelling. Here are some reasons why brand storytelling is important in content marketing:

❖ Humanizes your brand: A brand story gives your brand a

human face, making it more relatable to your audience by showcasing the people and values behind it.

❖ Builds trust and loyalty: By sharing a brand story that aligns with your audience's values and interests, you build trust and loyalty with them, fostering a long-term relationship.

❖ Differentiates your brand: A brand story that is unique, authentic, and memorable sets your brand apart from others in the market, elevating its position and enhancing its competitive advantage.

❖ Increases engagement: Brand storytelling evokes emotions, making your content more engaging and shareable, and increasing your chances of achieving virality.

Different Elements of Brand Storytelling

Before developing your brand story, it's important to understand the different elements that make up a compelling brand story. While each brand story is unique, they all share some common elements, including:

❖ The protagonist: The protagonist is the central character in your brand story. It's the hero that your audience can relate to and empathize with. Your brand could be the protagonist or a customer that your brand has helped.

❖ The conflict: Every good story has a conflict, and your brand story should be no exception. The conflict is the challenge or problem that your protagonist faces and how your brand helps them overcome it.

❖ The solution: The solution is how your brand solves the protagonist's problem, resolving the conflict and creating a positive outcome.

❖ The moral: The moral is the lesson or value that your story conveys to your audience. It's your brand's message and what it stands for.

How to Develop Your Brand Story

Developing a brand story takes time and effort, and it's a continuous process that evolves as your brand grows. Here are some tips on how to develop your brand story:

- ❖ Define your brand values: Your brand values are your guiding principles and beliefs that define your brand's personality. Identify what your brand stands for, what it cares about, and what it aims to achieve.

- ❖ Know your audience: Understand who your audience is, what they care about, and what motivates them. This helps you create a brand story that resonates with them.

- ❖ Be authentic: Your brand story must be authentic, genuine, and honest. Consumers can easily detect when a brand story is fabricated, so be true to your brand's personality and values.

- ❖ Keep it simple: Your brand story should be simple, concise, and easy to understand. Avoid using jargon and technical terms that can confuse your audience.

- ❖ Make it emotional: Brand stories that evoke emotions are more memorable and impactful. Use storytelling techniques such as metaphors, anecdotes, and humour to make your brand story more compelling.

Tips for Telling Compelling Brand Stories

Once you've developed your brand story, it's time to integrate it across all your marketing channels. Here are some tips for telling compelling brand stories:

- ❖ Use different formats: Brand stories can be told through various formats such as videos, blog posts, social media posts, podcasts, webinars, and infographics. Choose the format that resonates the most with your audience.

❖ Be consistent: Your brand story should be consistent across all your marketing channels, including your website, social media profiles, and email newsletters. This consistency helps build brand recognition and recall.

❖ Showcase your employees: Your employees are an integral part of your brand story. Showcase their stories and contributions to your brand's success through employee spotlights, interviews, and testimonials.

❖ Use customer stories: Customer stories are a powerful way to showcase how your brand has helped them overcome their challenges and achieve their goals.

❖ Incorporate visuals: Visuals such as images, videos, and infographics can enhance your brand story, making it more engaging and memorable.

The Role of Emotions in Brand Storytelling

Finally, emotions are at the heart of brand storytelling. Emotions are the driving force behind consumer behaviour, and by tapping into the right emotions, you can create a lasting connection with your audience. Here are some emotions that you can evoke through your brand story:

❖ Empathy: Evoke empathy by showcasing how your brand cares about its consumers and how it aims to make their lives better.

❖ Inspiration: Use your brand story to inspire your audience to take action, pursue their dreams, or make a positive impact.

❖ Trust: Build trust with your audience by sharing stories

that are genuine, honest, and transparent.

❖   Excitement: Create excitement by showcasing your brand's achievements, milestones, and innovations.

❖   Nostalgia: Use nostalgia to create an emotional connection with your audience, by reminding them of good memories and experiences.

Conclusion

Incorporating brand storytelling in your content marketing strategy can be a game-changer for your brand. By creating a unique, authentic, and compelling brand story, you can differentiate your brand from others in the market, build trust and loyalty with your audience, and increase engagement and virality. Remember to keep your brand story simple, authentic, and emotional, and integrate it across all your marketing channels consistently and creatively. By doing so, you can create a brand that resonates with your audience, and a lasting impact in the market.

CHAPTER 15: NURTURING YOUR LEADS WITH CONTENT

Lead nurturing is the process of building relationships with potential customers in order to turn them into paying customers. The process typically involves providing leads with valuable information at each stage of the buyer's journey. Effective lead nurturing strategies can significantly increase lead conversion rates and revenue.

In this chapter, we'll explore the different stages of the lead nurturing process and how to create effective lead nurturing content.

The Stages of the Lead Nurturing Process

There are several stages of the lead nurturing process, which include:

❖ Awareness Stage: In this stage, potential customers are just discovering your brand for the first time. Your goal is to attract their attention and provide them with helpful information that will encourage them to continue engaging with your brand.

❖ Interest Stage: In this stage, potential customers have demonstrated a sustained interest in your brand. Your goal is to provide them with more targeted information that matches their interests and pain points.

❖ Consideration Stage: In this stage, potential customers are actively considering making a purchase. Your goal is to provide them with detailed information about your products or services, answer their questions, and help them make a decision.

❖ Purchase Stage: In this stage, potential customers are ready to make a purchase. Your goal is to provide them with the information they need to complete the purchase and become a loyal customer.

Creating Effective Lead Nurturing Content

Creating effective lead nurturing content requires an understanding of your target audience's needs and interests at each stage of the buyer's journey. Here are some tips:

❖ Develop a content strategy: Create a plan for the type of content you will produce and how it will be delivered to potential customers at each stage of the buyer's journey.

❖ Use targeted messaging: Speak directly to prospects' pain points at each stage of the buyer's journey. Use messaging that is tailored to their specific needs and interests.

❖ Provide valuable information: Provide prospects with information that is useful and valuable. This will build trust and help establish your brand as an industry authority.

❖ Use multiple channels: Use multiple channels to deliver your content to potential customers, including email, social media, and your website.

❖ Use marketing automation: Use marketing automation tools to track prospects' behaviour and send them targeted content based on their interests and behaviour.

❖ Segment your leads: Segment leads based on their behaviour and interests, and send them content that is tailored to their unique needs.

❖ Measure and optimize: Measure the effectiveness of your lead nurturing campaigns, and optimize them based on the results. Continuously test and refine your content to improve results.

Conclusion

Lead nurturing is an essential part of any successful content marketing strategy. To create effective lead nurturing content, you must understand your target audience's needs and interests at each stage of the buyer's journey. Providing prospects with valuable information that addresses their pain points and nurtures them through the buyer's journey can significantly increase conversion rates and revenue. By using targeted messaging, multiple channels, marketing automation, segmentation, and continuous optimization, you can create an effective lead nurturing strategy that will help you build long-term relationships with your potential customers.

CHAPTER 16:
USING CONTENT
FOR CUSTOMER
RETENTION

One of the key areas of focus in content marketing is customer retention. It's a well-known fact that it's much easier and cheaper to retain customers than to acquire new ones, and effective content marketing can be a valuable tool for building customer loyalty.

In this chapter, we'll explore the different types of content you can use to retain customers, as well as tips and strategies for creating effective retention content.

Importance of Customer Retention in Content Marketing

Many businesses place a heavy emphasis on acquisition-focused marketing strategies, such as SEO, social media advertising, and PPC campaigns. While these are all important tactics for driving traffic and acquiring new customers, they don't always prioritize the customer experience after the initial sale.

Customer retention, on the other hand, is all about building long-term relationships with your customers and keeping them engaged with your brand. This can help to increase customer lifetime value, reduce churn rates, and create brand advocates who will promote your business to others.

Different Types of Content for Customer Retention

To effectively retain customers, you need to provide them with valuable and engaging content that will keep them coming back for more. Some of the most effective types of retention content include:

❖ Educational content: Providing your customers with helpful and informative content can keep them engaged and interested in your brand. This could include how-to articles or videos, tutorials, or e-books that help your customers better understand your products or services.

❖ Support content: Support content can help your customers troubleshoot common issues or problems with your product or service. This could include FAQs, troubleshooting guides, or support forums where customers can ask questions and receive assistance.

❖ Promotional content: While promotional content is less common for customer retention, it can still be effective if used sparingly. For example, sending exclusive offers or discounts to your existing customers can show them that you value their business and encourage repeat purchases.

❖ Personalized content: Personalization is becoming increasingly important in content marketing, and it can be just as valuable for customer retention. Tailoring your content to your customers' interests, behaviours, and preferences can help to build a deeper connection with them and improve the overall customer experience.

How to Create Effective Retention Content

Creating effective retention content requires a different mindset than acquisition-focused content. Instead of trying to attract new customers, you're looking to engage and retain existing ones. Here are some tips for creating effective retention content:

1. Focus on the customer: Your retention content should be centred around the needs and interests of your customers. Consider what types of content would be most valuable to them, and tailor your content strategy accordingly.

2. Use the right channels: The channels you use to distribute your content can have a big impact on its effectiveness. Consider where your customers are most active and engaged, and make sure your content is optimized for those channels.

3. Keep it fresh: Don't just rely on the same types of content over and over again. Keep your retention content fresh and varied by experimenting with different formats and topics.

4. Personalize where possible: If you have the data to personalize your content, use it! Personalized content can help to improve engagement and keep your customers interested in your brand.

Tips for Keeping Your Customers Engaged

Creating great retention content is just the first step. To keep your customers engaged and coming back for more, you need to stay top-of-mind and provide ongoing value. Here are some tips for keeping your customers engaged:

- ❖ Stay in touch: Regularly communicate with your customers through email newsletters, social media updates, or other channels. This will help to keep them up-to-date on new products or services, and show that you're invested in their ongoing experience with your brand.

- ❖ Encourage feedback: Encouraging your customers to provide feedback can help you improve your products or services, and also make them feel valued and heard. Consider using surveys, feedback forms, or other mechanisms to gather feedback from your customers.

❖ Offer support: Providing responsive and helpful customer support is essential for retaining customers. Make sure you have the resources and processes in place to quickly address any issues or problems your customers may encounter.

❖ Create a sense of community: Building a sense of community among your customers can help to create a deeper connection with your brand. Consider creating a forum or social media group where customers can connect and engage with each other.

How to Measure the Success of Your Retention Content

To evaluate the effectiveness of your retention content, you need to track relevant metrics and analyse the impact of your efforts. Here are some key metrics to consider when measuring the success of your retention content:

❖ Churn rate: Your churn rate is the percentage of customers who stop doing business with you over a given period of time. Lower churn rates indicate higher customer retention and satisfaction.

❖ Repeat purchase rate: The repeat purchase rate shows how frequently your customers make repeat purchases. This is a key indicator of customer loyalty and engagement.

❖ Engagement rate: Your engagement rate measures how often your customers engage with your retention content. This could include clicks, opens, views, or other actions depending on the type of content.

❖ Customer satisfaction: Tracking customer satisfaction through surveys or other mechanisms can help you understand how well your retention content is serving your customers' needs.

The Benefits of Retention Content for Customer Loyalty

Effective retention content can have a powerful impact on customer loyalty and retention. By providing ongoing value and engaging your customers beyond the initial sale, you can build a deeper connection with your audience and create brand advocates who are more likely to recommend your business to others.

Retention content also has the potential to increase customer lifetime value by encouraging repeat purchases and reducing churn rates. Ultimately, a strong retention content strategy can help you build a thriving and sustainable business over the long-term.

Summary

In this chapter, we explored how to use content marketing for customer retention. Effective retention content can help to build customer loyalty, increase customer lifetime value, and create brand advocates who will promote your business to others. We discussed key types of retention content, such as educational, support, promotional, and personalized content, as well as tips for creating effective retention content. Additionally, we covered strategies for keeping customers engaged and measuring the success of your retention content, as well as the benefits of retention content for customer loyalty.

CHAPTER 17: CREATING CONTENT FOR SEO

Search engine optimization, more commonly known as SEO, is an essential part of any successful content marketing strategy. SEO enables you to increase your website's visibility in search engine results and drive organic traffic to your site. In this chapter, we'll discuss the basics of SEO, as well as tips and tricks for creating content that is optimized for search engines.

How Search Engines Work:

Before we delve into creating SEO-friendly content, it's essential to understand how search engines work. The primary function of a search engine is to provide users with the most relevant and valuable results based on their search queries.

To do this, search engines use algorithms that analyse a variety of factors, including keywords, website structure, and backlinks, among others, to determine which sites are the most relevant and useful for a particular search query.

Therefore, to optimize your content for search engines, you need to understand these algorithms and make sure your content meets the criteria they are looking for.

How to Conduct Keyword Research:

Keyword research is a crucial step in creating SEO-friendly content. Keywords are the words and phrases that people use to search for information online. By understanding the keywords your target audience is using, you can create content that aligns with their search queries and increases your website's visibility in search results.

To conduct keyword research, you can use tools like Google's Keyword Planner and SEMrush. These tools will help you identify relevant keywords for your niche and show you the search volume, competition, and other relevant metrics for each keyword.

Once you've identified your keywords, you can use them strategically in your content to optimize it for search engines. However, be sure to avoid "keyword stuffing," which is the practice of overusing keywords in your content in an attempt to manipulate rankings. Google's algorithms are designed to penalize sites that engage in this practice, so focus on creating high-quality content that incorporates keywords naturally and provides value to your target audience.

Tips for Writing Content for SEO:

When it comes to creating SEO-friendly content, there are several strategies you can use to ensure your content ranks well in search engine results.

- ❖ Focus on high-quality content: The first and most important step in creating SEO-friendly content is to produce high-quality content that provides value to your target audience. This content should be informative, engaging, and relevant to the keywords you want to rank for.

- ❖ Incorporate keywords strategically: As mentioned earlier, keywords are essential for SEO. Incorporate them strategically in your content, including your headlines, subheadings, and body text without overdoing it.

❖   Use a descriptive URL: Another way to optimize your content for search engines is by using a descriptive URL that includes your target keyword. This not only helps search engines understand what your content is about, but it also makes it easier for users to remember and share your content.

❖   Optimize your images: Images can also help improve your SEO. Be sure to use alt tags and descriptive file names to help search engines understand what your images are about.

❖   Use internal linking: Internal linking is the practice of linking to other pages on your website. This helps search engines understand the structure of your site and can improve your rankings.

❖   Build high-quality backlinks: Backlinks are links from other websites that point to your site. The more high-quality backlinks you have, the more likely it is that search engines will rank your site higher in search results. But be careful to avoid purchasing or building backlinks using shady practices, which can harm your rankings.

How to Measure and Improve Your SEO Performance:

To measure the success of your SEO efforts, you'll need to track your keyword rankings, website traffic, and backlinks, among other metrics. Google Analytics and SEMrush are both great tools for tracking these metrics.

One effective way to improve your SEO performance is by creating and implementing a content calendar that includes a mix of evergreen content and time-sensitive content that targets keywords with high search volume and low competition.

Additionally, keep track of your website's loading speed, mobile-friendliness, and other technical factors that can impact your SEO. Google's algorithm prioritizes sites that load quickly and are mobile-friendly, so make sure your site checks these boxes.

In summary, optimizing your content for SEO is critical if you want to drive organic traffic to your website. Conducting keyword research, incorporating keywords strategically, creating high-quality content, using a descriptive URL, optimizing your images, using internal linking, and building high-quality backlinks can all help improve your SEO rankings. Tracking and analysing your SEO metrics regularly and staying up-to-date on SEO best practices is also crucial for continued success.

CHAPTER 18: CREATING CONTENT FOR EMAIL MARKETING

Email marketing is a powerful tool for content marketing. It allows you to reach a wide audience, build relationships with them, and drive conversions. In this chapter, we will discuss the different types of email marketing content, tips for writing effective emails, and the benefits of email marketing for lead nurturing.

Types of Email Marketing Content

There are different types of email marketing content that you can create, including:

1. Newsletters: These are regular emails that provide subscribers with updates on your brand, products, and services. You can also include relevant industry news, tips, and resources.

2. Promotional Emails: These emails promote your products and services. You can use them to announce new products, offer discounts, or encourage subscribers to make a purchase.

3. Event Invitations: These emails invite subscribers to attend a webinar or physical event.

4. Welcome Emails: These are emails that are sent to new subscribers to welcome them to your list and introduce them to your brand.

5. Educational Emails: These emails provide subscribers with educational content such as blog posts, ebooks, and tutorials.

Effective Email Copywriting Tips

To ensure that your emails are effective, you need to focus on copywriting. Here are some tips for writing effective email copy:

❖ Grab attention with the subject line: The subject line is the first thing that subscribers will see. It needs to be catchy and relevant to encourage subscribers to open the email.

❖ Keep it short and simple: Emails should be concise and easy to read. Keep paragraphs short, use bulleted lists, and avoid complicated language.

❖ Use personalization: Address subscribers by their names, and use personalization based on their behaviour and preferences.

❖ Include a clear call-to-action: Every email should have a clear call-to-action (CTA). The CTA should be prominent and easy to understand.

❖ Test and optimize: Test different subject lines, copy, and CTAs to see what works best. Analyse your email metrics to optimize your email marketing strategy.

Benefits of Email Marketing for Lead Nurturing

Email marketing is an effective tool for lead nurturing. Here are some benefits of email marketing for lead nurturing:

❖ Increased engagement: Email marketing allows you to engage with your leads on a regular basis. By providing them with valuable content, you can build relationships with them and keep them interested in your brand.

❖ Personalization: Email marketing allows you to personalize your communication with your leads. You can segment your list and send targeted emails based on their interests and behaviour.

❖ Lead scoring: By analysing your email metrics, you can score your leads based on their engagement. This allows you to identify high-quality leads that are more likely to convert.

❖ Lead nurturing automation: There are many tools available that allow you to automate your lead nurturing process. This saves time and ensures that your leads are receiving relevant content at the right time.

❖ Improved conversion rates: Effective lead nurturing through email marketing can result in improved conversion rates. By building relationships with your leads and providing them with valuable content, you can encourage them to take action.

Conclusion

Email marketing is a powerful tool for content marketing. By creating different types of email marketing content and using effective copywriting techniques, you can engage with your audience and build relationships with them. Email marketing is also an effective tool for lead nurturing, allowing you to personalize your communication and improve your conversion rates.

CHAPTER 19: STAYING AHEAD OF THE GAME

In a constantly evolving landscape such as content marketing, it is essential to keep up with trends and best practices to stay ahead of the game. The digital marketing world is never static, as new tools and strategies are consistently being introduced, and staying informed is critical. With that in mind, this chapter explores how to stay up-to-date on content marketing to keep your business ahead of the competition.

Importance of Keeping Up with Trends and Best Practices

Being current on the latest trends and industry best practices can drastically impact your success in content marketing. In addition, staying updated on the latest developments in your niche helps you ensure that your content resonates with your target audience. Following the latest trends in your industry guides you to make informed decisions in creating content that generates leads and conversions.

Different Ways to Stay Up-to-Date on Content Marketing

The good news is that there are many resources available for staying up-to-date with the latest content marketing trends and best practices. You can follow influencers and thought leaders in your industry on social media platforms like LinkedIn, Twitter, and YouTube, who regularly post about new developments and insights on the latest marketing trends. Additionally, there are podcasts, blogs, newsletters, and webinars dedicated to covering the latest developments and thought leadership in the industry.

How to Analyse and Learn from Your Competitors

Competitor analysis is an important component of learning from the competition. Analysing your competitors' content marketing strategies can offer insights into how you should position your brand in the industry. When assessing your competitors, try to determine best practices such as the type, frequency, and quality of content that resonates with their target audience.

The Role of Innovation in Content Marketing

Innovation drives the successful implementation of a content marketing strategy. Innovation is crucial for staying ahead of the competition as it helps brands create unique and high-quality content that resonates with their target audience. Innovation also provides a competitive advantage in an ever-changing marketplace.

Tips for Continuously Improving Your Content Marketing Strategy

One way to continue improving your content marketing strategy is by gathering, analysing and implementing data-driven insights. Analysing metrics such as engagement rates, click-through rates, and conversions on different pieces of content can offer valuable insights on how to improve future campaigns. Conducting data analysis helps brands identify strengths in their content marketing strategy and opportunities for improvement. Continuously experimenting, testing and iterating is another sure way of refining your marketing plan and staying ahead.

How to Stay Ahead of the Competition

To stay ahead of the competition in content marketing, you need to always be aware of the latest developments and trends in your industry, consistently analyse your competition, and remain innovative with your messaging and content offerings to your audience. A learning mindset is essential in a constantly evolving landscape such as content marketing, so one must always be ready to make adjustments as needed.

The Importance of Cultivating a Learning Mindset

Cultivating a learning mindset is vital in the highly dynamic landscape of content marketing. The ability to quickly adapt and pivot a strategy is essential in a world of changing trends and algorithms. As content marketing continues to evolve, the ability to learn and evolve with it is one of the most valuable traits for a marketer.

Summary

Staying ahead of the game in content marketing requires staying up-to-date on the latest trends and best practices through resources like podcasts, blogs, newsletters, and webinars. Analysing the competition, innovating, and continuously improving your content marketing strategy is also critical. Cultivating a learning mindset is key to success in a constantly evolving industry.

CHAPTER 20:
CONCLUSION

Congratulations! If you have made it to this chapter, you have gained insight into the secrets of successful content marketing. You understand the importance of creating and distributing great content that resonates with your audience. You know how to set clear goals, measure your results and make data-driven decisions. And most importantly, you are well-equipped to leverage content marketing as a powerful tool to grow your business.

Here is a recap of the key points we covered in this book:

In Chapter 1, we discussed the importance of content marketing in digital marketing and provided an overview of the different types of content marketing. We also looked at successful content marketing campaigns and the benefits and challenges of content marketing.

In Chapter 2, we explained the importance of audience research and how to create audience personas. We also provided useful tips for tailoring content to your audience.

Chapter 3 focused on developing a content strategy, outlining the steps for creating an effective strategy that aligns with your business goals.

Chapter 4 delved into the characteristics of compelling content and provided tips for brainstorming content ideas, writing effective headlines and titles, and optimizing your content for search engines.

In Chapter 5, we discussed the importance of content distribution and the different channels for content distribution. We shared tips for amplifying your content reach and leveraging social media for content distribution.

In Chapter 6, we went over the importance of measuring content performance and discussed the key metrics to track. We also showed how to analyse your content metrics, test your content and continuously improve your content performance.

Chapter 7 explored the importance of repurposing your content, and provided different ways to repurpose content, and the benefits of repurposing content for SEO.

Chapter 8 discussed the importance of having a successful blog and shared tips for creating engaging blog posts, optimizing your blog for search engines, and promoting your blog.

Chapter 9 demonstrated the importance of video in content marketing and explored different types of video content and how to create, edit, and promote videos.

Chapter 10 outlined the importance of thought leadership in content marketing and provided tips for creating thought leadership content and promoting your thought leadership.

In Chapter 11, we dove into user-generated content and provided tips for encouraging and managing user-generated content.

Chapter 12 examined the importance of social media in content marketing and provided tips for creating engaging social media posts, optimizing your social media profiles, and using social media advertising.

Chapter 13 discussed the importance of interactive content and provided tips for creating engaging interactive content.

Chapter 14 explored brand storytelling in content marketing

and provided guidelines for developing a brand story, telling compelling brand stories, and integrating brand storytelling across all marketing channels.

Chapter 15 and Chapter 16 explored creating content for lead nurturing and customer retention respectively. Both of these chapters provided useful tips for creating the right content at the right time to keep your leads engaged and customers loyal to your brand.

Chapter 17 focused specifically on creating content for SEO, examining key concepts like search engine algorithms and keyword research.

Chapter 18 explored creating content for email marketing and provided tips for writing effective email copy, designing engaging emails, personalizing your emails, and measuring your email metrics.

In Chapter 19, we discussed the importance of staying ahead of the game in content marketing and provided tips for staying up-to-date on trends, analysing and learning from your competitors, and continuously improving your own content marketing strategies.

In conclusion, when it comes to content marketing, there are no shortcuts. Consistency and persistence are key to success. Creating great content and distributing it to the right channels can build trust with your audience, establish thought leadership and drive business growth. If you implement the tips and strategies provided in this book, you will be well on your way to mastering content marketing and achieving the results you desire.

Final Thoughts

I truly hope that this book has provided you with valuable insights into the world of content marketing, and has given you the tools and strategies you need to create compelling content that resonates with your target audience.

One of the most important things to keep in mind when it comes to content marketing is that it's not a one-size-fits-all approach. Every business is unique, and therefore requires a unique approach to their content marketing strategy. It's important to experiment and try different tactics until you find what works best for your business.

Remember, creating high-quality content is just one piece of the puzzle. You also need to make sure that your content is distributed effectively across multiple channels, such as social media, email newsletters, and paid advertising platforms.

Finally, don't forget about the importance of analytics. Regularly monitoring your metrics will allow you to see what's working and what's not, so that you can adjust your strategy accordingly.

Thank you for reading Content Marketing Secrets. I wish you all the best in your future content marketing endeavours!

ABOUT THE AUTHOR

Ray Goodwin

Ray Goodwin, is the author behind this series of captivating books on Business Development and self improvement, and has left an indelible mark on the field. He was born and raised in the bustling city of London, where he developed a strong work ethic and an insatiable curiosity about the inner workings of successful businesses. Throughout his illustrious career, Ray leveraged his extensive knowledge and experience to help numerous companies flourish and prosper.

His keen insights and innovative strategies has earned him recognition, driving him to share his expertise with others. Ray believes in the power of sharing knowledge to elevate businesses and empower aspiring entrepreneurs.

Ray's dedication to his craft is evident in the numerous books he has authored on business development and self improvement. His writing style seamlessly blends practical advice, thought-provoking concepts, and real-life case studies, making his books invaluable resources for business professionals and novices alike. His ability to distill complex concepts into accessible language has greatly impacted the lives and careers of countless individuals.

Now retired from the corporate world, Ray and his beloved wife have settled in the idyllic English countryside. Surrounded by the beauty of nature, Ray finds inspiration for his writing and indulges in his hobbies.

Ray Goodwin's books continue to serve as enduring guides for those seeking success in the business world. With a wealth of experience and a deep understanding of the inner workings of businesses, Ray's work remains a testament to his passion for sharing knowledge and helping others flourish.

www.ingramcontent.com/pod-product-compliance
Lightning Source LLC
Chambersburg PA
CBHW062342290526
45794CB00005B/2079